Amazing Animals
of the
Rainforest

Danny Pearson

WOW! facts

Badger Publishing Limited
Oldmedow Road,
Hardwick Industrial Estate,
King's Lynn PE30 4JJ
Telephone: 01438 791037

www.badgerlearning.co.uk

2 4 6 8 10 9 7 5 3

Amazing Animals of the Rainforest ISBN 978-1-78464-002-6

Text © Danny Pearson 2014

Complete work © Badger Publishing Limited 2014

Publisher: Susan Ross
Senior Editor: Danny Pearson
Publishing Assistant: Claire Morgan
Designer: Fiona Grant
Series Consultant: Dee Reid

Photos: Cover Image: © Picture Press/Alamy
Page 5: © Radius Images / Alamy
Page 7: Mint Images/REX
Page 8: © Carlos Mora/Alamy
Page 9: © Nigel Dickinson/Alamy
Page 10: © Papilio/Alamy
Page 11: FLPA/REX
Page 12: © William Mullins/Alamy
Page 13: © Ryan M. Bolton/Alamy
Page 14: © Morley Read/Alamy
Page 15: Glenn Bartley/Getty Images
Page 16: © National Geographic Image Collection/Alamy
Page 17: Image Broker/REX, © All Canada Photos/Alamy
Page 18: iqbalsiddiqui/Getty Images
Page 19: Nature Picture Library/REX
Page 20: © Maximilian Weinzierl/Alamy
Page 21: FLPA/REX
Page 22: Jean-Luc Brouard/Robert Harding/REX
Page 23: Image Broker/REX
Page 24: FLPA/REX
Page 25: Design Pics Inc/REX
Page 26: FLPA/REX
Page 27: © BRUCE COLEMAN INC./Alamy
Page 28: © Nature Picture Library/Alamy
Page 29: FLPA/Hugh Lansdown/REX
Page 30: © blickwinkel/Alamy

Attempts to contact all copyright holders have been made.
If any omitted would care to contact Badger Learning, we will be happy to make appropriate arrangements.

Contents

Vocabulary

amphibian

axolotl

camouflage

capybara

chameleon

deforestation

pygmy marmoset

venomous

1. The rainforest

Rainforests are home to some of the most amazing animals in the world.

There are rainforests all across the world but the largest rainforests are in South America.

In a rainforest the weather is very hot and very wet.

Over half of all the plants and animals of the world live in rainforests but the rainforest covers less than 10% of the Earth's surface.

Rainforests of the world

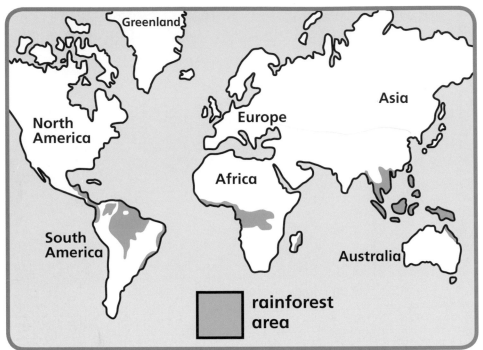

All of these foods originally come from the rainforest:

- bananas
- cocoa
- sugar
- coffee

Nearly 80% of the vegetables and fruit we eat were first found in rainforests.

New types of animals are being discovered in the rainforest all the time.

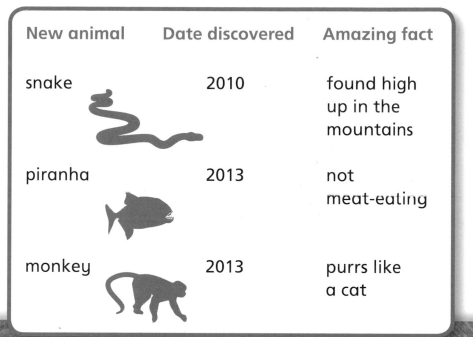

New animal	Date discovered	Amazing fact
snake	2010	found high up in the mountains
piranha	2013	not meat-eating
monkey	2013	purrs like a cat

But due to deforestation, around 137 plant, animal and insect species are wiped out every day!

People in the rainforest

Animals and plants are not the only living things in the rainforests.

People live in rainforests, too. They are very skilled at getting fruit that grows on the trees and hunting the animals and fish.

Sadly, some people see rainforests as a place to make money.

Big companies cut down the trees and sell the timber.

When the trees are cut down, the animals lose their habitat and many die.

In the Amazon, an area the size of Wales is cut down almost every year.

2 Insects

The Goliath beetle is the world's largest beetle. It can grow up to 15 centimetres long.

Each of the beetle's legs has a hook on the end of it to help it climb.

The male Goliath beetle has a Y-shaped horn on its head. It uses the horn to fight other males.

This odd insect is called the giraffe weevil. It is called the giraffe weevil because of its long neck.

The female uses her long neck to roll up a leaf to make a nest. Then she lays a single egg in the nest.

Ants

The rainforest is home to many different types of ant.

As many as 200 different kinds of ant can be found on one tree.

The bullet ant is the largest and the most feared because of the bite it can give. The pain is said to be the same as being shot, which is how the ant got its name.

WOW! facts

Some tribes use bullet ants in ceremonies where boys are stung. The boys have to put their hand into a glove full of bullet ants and leave it there for ten minutes! If they do not cry then they have proved they are warriors.

Spiders

The most venomous spider is the Brazilian wandering spider.

Its venom can kill a man in 20 minutes. It is a big spider and its body can be five centimetres long with a leg span of 15 centimetres.

The Brazilian wandering spider is also called the banana spider and has been found in the UK in boxes of bananas. So watch out next time you eat a banana!

3. Birds

This odd-looking bird is called a potoo.

It lives in the rainforest. Its big yellow eyes and big beak help it to feed at night on insects.

In the daytime it sits still on a branch. Its brown and green feathers makes it look like tree bark.

One of the most famous birds living in rainforests is the blue bird of paradise.

The male birds hang upside-down and show off their colourful feathers to attract females.

Toucans have very long, sharp beaks. Their beaks can grow up to half their body length.

They use their sharp beaks to squash fruit and berries but also to kill smaller birds.

Macaws are the largest type of parrot. They have a sharp, hooked beak for eating nuts, fruit and seeds.

4. Mammals

The world's largest bat is the flying fox. Its wing span is almost two metres. It only eats fruit.

The smallest bat is the bumble bee bat. It weighs less than a one pence coin and is the same size as a bumble bee, which is how it got its name.

The okapi has a long neck like a giraffe and stripes like a zebra. It lives in the African rainforest.

When these animals were first discovered many people did not believe that they were real.

In large rivers in the rainforests you may find the pink dolphin.

Unlike sea dolphins, the pink dolphin has a hump on its back instead of a fin.

Pink dolphins feed on fish but they will also eat turtles and crabs.

The largest rat on the planet lives in the rainforest.
It is called a capybara.

It can grow to over a metre long.

A capybara can run fast and it can stay under water
for five minutes.

Sloths

Sloths are very slow animals. They spend most of their lives hanging in trees and can sleep for up to 16 hours a day.

They usually only come down from the trees once a week to do a poo!

There are two types of sloth, the three-toed sloth and the two-toed sloth.

The fur on a sloth grows backwards because it is upside-down hanging from trees for most of its life. This helps rainwater to flow off its body easily.

WOW! facts

Although sloths are very slow animals, they are good swimmers.

The loudest monkey in the world is the black howler monkey.

When a troop of these monkeys starts howling, the noise can be heard three miles away.

The smallest monkey in the world is the pygmy marmoset.

It is only 12 centimetres tall and can fit into your hand.

You might think this monkey would make a cute pet but if it doesn't like you it will give you a sharp bite and throw its poo at you!

WOW! facts

The pygmy marmoset's tail is longer than its body.

5. More amazing animals

The chameleon is famous for its camouflage. It can change the colour of its skin to blend in with its background.

This helps it to hide from other animals.

WOW! facts

A chameleon can change colour in under 20 seconds!

The axolotl is called the walking fish. It isn't really a fish, it's an amphibian.

It spends its time walking on its four legs under water.

WOW! facts

If an axolotl loses one of its legs, a new leg grows in its place!

One of the world's strangest-looking frogs is the glass frog.

You can see right through its body. This allows the frog to blend in with its background, making it very hard to see.

The poison dart frog is brightly coloured. These bright colours warn other animals that it does not taste very nice and they should leave it alone.

WOW! facts

Poison dart frogs are the most toxic animals on Earth.

The aye aye lemur is a very strange-looking animal.

It has large eyes that help it to see in the dark.

It uses its one very long finger to dig out insects from trees.

Questions

Why is the bullet ant feared so much? *(page 13)*

What is the name of the world's smallest bat? *(page 18)*

How is the pink dolphin different from regular dolphins? *(page 20)*

What are the names of the two types of sloth that are found in rainforests? *(page 22)*

What is the loudest monkey on Earth called? *(page 24)*

What is the most toxic animal on the planet? *(page 29)*

Index